SNOWBOARDING

First American edition published in 2004
by LernerSports

This book is available in two editions:
Library binding by LernerSports
Soft cover by First Avenue Editions
Imprints of Lerner Publishing Group
241 First Avenue North
Minneapolis, MN 55401 U.S.A.

Website address: www.lernerbooks.com

Designed and produced by:
David West 👫 **Children's Books**
7 Princeton Court
55 Felsham Road
London, England

Designer: Gary Jeffrey
Editor: James Pickering
Picture Research: Carlotta Cooper

Library of Congress Cataloging-in-Publication Data

Barr, Matt.
  Snowboarding / by Matt Barr & Chris Moran. –
1st American ed.
    p. cm.—(Extreme sports)
  Includes index.
  Summary: Discusses the history of snowboarding,
some of the sport's pioneers, techniques and styles,
necessary equipment, popular resorts, dangers, and
more.
  ISBN: 0–8225–1242–4 (lib. bdg.)
  ISBN: 0–8225–1192–4 (pbk.)
  1. Snowboarding–Juvenile literature. [1.
Snowboarding.] I. Moran, Chris. II. Title. III.
Extreme Sports (Minneapolis, Minn.)
  GV857.S57 B37 2004
  769.9—dc21
Bound in the United States of America
1 2 3 4 5 6 – OS – 09 08 07 06 05 04

*An explanation of difficult words can be
found in the glossary on page 31.*

extreme sports

SNOWBOARDING

Matt Barr & Chris Moran

LERNER
SPORTS
AN IMPRINT OF LERNER PUBLISHING GROUP

CONTENTS

Introduction

Nobody really knows when snowboarding began. Paintings in Norway show that people may have used snowboards for transportation even before skis were invented. Early snowboards definitely existed in the 1920s. As a sport, snowboarding became popular in the 1970s and 1980s. By the 1990s, it was huge.

Snowboarding lets you discover some of the world's most beautiful and adventurous mountains. Like its cousins skateboarding and surfing, snowboarding is popular for many reasons. Freedom and excitement are the two most important.

FLYING THROUGH THE AIR
Dropping off of cliffs and launching off jumps are some of snowboarding's biggest thrills.

TURNING THROUGH NEWLY FALLEN SNOW
Fresh powder is what every snowboarder dreams of.

WARNING!
SNOWBOARDING CAN BE AN **EXTREMELY DANGEROUS** SPORT. DO NOT TRY ANY FORM OF SNOWBOARDING WITHOUT **ADULT SUPERVISION**.

In 1965 Sherman Poppen, an American chemical engineer, mixed skiing and surfing to invent the Snurfer. He made the toy as a gift for his daughter Wendy. But within a year, about 500,000 Snurfers had been sold across the United States.

SNURFING!
A 1960s ad

The Do-It-Yourself Years

The Snurfer gave other people the idea of surfing on snow. Throughout the 1970s, Tom Sims, Mike Olsen, Chuck Barfoot, and Jake Burton Carpenter adapted the Snurfer and invented their own boards. Thanks to them, the snowboarding business grew very quickly.

DO IT YOURSELF
Regis Rolland built his early boards from scratch.

EARLY BOARDS
These snowboards show how technology progressed from the early sled to high-tech modern boards.

Jake Burton Carpenter—the Father of Snowboarding?

Jake Burton Carpenter received a Snurfer at age 14. He soon began to make his own versions of the toy. In 1977 he moved to Vermont and set up Burton Snowboards. Jake helped get snowboarding recognized as a sport by ski areas. Burton Snowboards is the most successful snowboard company in the world.

JAKE BURTON CARPENTER
Carpenter still rides over 100 days a year and runs his company.

SNOWBOARDING SLANG

bail: to crash-land

bone: to grab the board and extend one leg to emphasize the quality of the trick

duckfoot: a stance where both feet point outward like a duck

fakie: boarding backward

grommet: a young super-hyped snowboarder

hucker: a rider without any style, who never "stomps" any tricks

jib: to ride something that's not snow, like a railing or a bench

kicker: a human-made snow ramp

leash: a device that attaches the board to your front leg

lifties: snowpark attendants

pow: fresh powder snow

shred: to snowboard

stomp: to land a trick solidly

switchstance: *see fakie*

toe drag: riders with big feet and narrow boards must drag their toes

7

Snowboarding's Evolution

In the late 1970s and 1980s, young boarders popped up all over the United States and Europe. In 1979 Mark Anolik found a natural half-pipe while snowboarding around Lake Tahoe, California. A half-pipe is a sloping ramp with a vertical edge.

The Early Lake Tahoe Scene

Word of Anolik's discovery spread. By 1981 future legends like Terry Kidwell and Tom Sims were often on the half-pipe. They were inventing freestyle snowboarding by using their skateboarding skills on snow.

TERRY KIDWELL
The father of modern freestyle

Europe: Regis Rolland and *Apocalypse Snow*

Meanwhile, in Europe, a similar group started in Les Arcs, France. Local Regis Rolland filmed himself and his friends for the hilarious *Apocalypse Snow* videos. The friends outran avalanches and showed off incredible snowboarding skills.

AMAZING STUNTS
Regis's films were totally crazy.

Nose Grab

Rocket

Crail

Japan

Lien

Indy

Mute

Method

Stalefish

Meloncollie

Tail Grab

GRABS

Grabs are the basis of freestyle snowboarding. Riders use them for more stability in the air. Grabs also show a snowboarder's style and board control. Almost every grab was originally invented on a skateboard and later adopted by snowboarders.

Rear hand grabs for a regular rider

Front hand grabs for a regular rider

Food Names and Style

The riders who invent grabs often give them strange names. Some names, like the Roast Beef, are inspired by food. But the origins of some others, like Stalefish, Indy, and Mute are much less clear.

The Method

Although the Method was originally a skateboarding trick, it has become very popular on snow, too. It's a graceful trick that involves bending your knees backward and twisting around to grab the center of the board between the bindings.

9

Equipment

The development of snowboarding equipment has always been led by those who know the most-the riders.

Snowboards

In the early days, boards were little more than sleds. They had no edges or strap bindings. Since then, boards have grown and shrunk. Metal edges and rounded tails and noses have become standard. Most modern snowboards look similar.

GLOVES
Snowboard gloves keep your hands warm and dry.

BOARDS

This is a modern-day snowboard. The similar shape at the front and back lets you ride it backward as easily as forward.

BOOTS
Snowboarding boots provide comfort, warmth, and ankle support.

ATTACHMENTS
Bindings attach to the board with screws via a central disk.

BINDINGS
Bindings hold the rider to the board. Easy to attach and remove, they offer the rider several ways to place his or her feet.

HELMET

Helmets are required in many snowparks. They protect your head during icy landings and accidents.

JACKET

Jackets should be waterproof and windproof.

GOGGLES

Goggles protect your eyes from snow, wind, and the sun's rays.

GUIDE #2

FASHION

Over the years, snowboarding has had more than its fair share of fashion crimes. In the 1980s, it was neon. In the 1990s, riders dyed their hair and wore clothes twice their normal size. Modern styling has settled down into a mix of fashion and function.

Resorts

It's possible to go snowboarding every day of the year. For many riders, this opportunity to travel and experience other cultures is one of the sport's biggest attractions.

VANCOUVER WHISTLER

Where Shall We Ride?

Most of the best snowboarders come from the United States, Canada, Scandinavia, and France. But snowboarding has become a global sport. Some of the world's best riders are from surprising places.

WHISTLER
Expect powder and amazing fun-parks at this resort in British Columbia, Canada. Many super-pro riders live here.

MAMMOTH
Mammoth has one of the best terrain parks in the world. This mountain in California is popular with freestyle riders.

BRECKENRIDGE
This high altitude resort in Colorado has huge, wide-groomed pistes (trails). Breckenridge is a favorite with families and beginners.

ALASKA
This northern state is home to the most extreme snowboarding in the world. Dry sea air, huge amounts of snow, and steep mountains produce unique conditions. Most of the resorts are accessible only with a helicopter. A guide is a must.

HEMSEDAL
Hemsedal hosts Norway's Spring Kicker Session each May.

THE HIMALAYAS
These mountains in Asia are difficult to reach. Amazing first descents and powder reward the willing.

NAGANO
Host of the 1998 Olympic Winter Games, Nagano, Japan, receives tons of snow each year.

LAS LEÑAS
Las Leñas boasts lots of snowfall and incredible natural terrain. It's popular for freeriding.

THREDBO
Thredbo is at the center of the fast-growing Australian scene.

TREBLE CONE
Heli-boarding, pipes, and parks are all popular in New Zealand.

SURF
INTERDIT

THE OUTLAWED SPORT?
Back in the 1970s and 1980s, many ski resorts banned snowboarding. They didn't like the attitude of some snowboarders. But these days snowboarders are welcomed at almost every resort in the world.

Basic Techniques

Compared to skiing, surfing, and skateboarding, snowboarding is pretty easy to pick up. The movements are fairly natural and stay the same, whatever your level. But you must learn the basics to achieve snowboarding glory.

1. Keep your knees bent. Relax your upper body.

2. Lean on your toe edge. The board will "carve" through the turn. Use your arms and upper body for balance.

3. Keep looking forward, not at your board.

4. To turn back the other way, push against the edge you're on. Then, using your upper body, start your turn.

5. Stand back upright from the toeside turn. Begin to switch your edge from toe to heel.

How to Turn and Stop

Turning and stopping are the basics of snowboarding. Luckily, they're simple to master. Practice linking your turns. Your journey from the top of the slope to the bottom should be one smooth, flowing ride.

GUIDE #3

EVEN MORE BASICS

Snowboarding can be frustrating at first. Lessons with a qualified instructor help a lot. Make sure your board, boots, and bindings are designed for beginners. Don't be afraid to wear pads on your knees, elbows, and backside.

Learning is easy with the right equipment.

6. You should be on your heel edge. By lifting and lowering your toes, you can carve through the heelside turn as gently or as hard as you like.

REGULAR OR GOOFY?

As you stand sideways on your board, decide whether you prefer your left foot forward (regular) or your right (goofy).

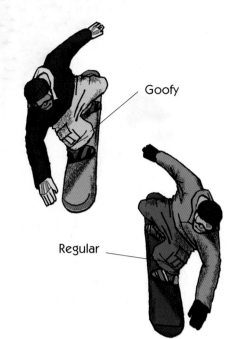

Goofy

Regular

7. You are completely "on an edge."

8. It's time to turn back to your toeside edge. Change from your heel edge to your toe edge. If all has gone well, you should be back to the start of the diagram.

15

Terrain

Once you've got those awkward beginner days out of the way, the mountain becomes your playground. The search for new places to ride is only limited by your imagination and snowboarding safety.

Piste

Pistes are the marked trails that crisscross every resort. They offer the safest means of getting around. Huge machines groom the pistes each night. Hitting a piste early in the morning is one of snowboarding's simplest pleasures.

ON PISTE
Pistes are smooth, specially-made runs.

A PISTE MAP
A resort map marking the pistes

OFF-PISTE
With a bit of exploring, huge powder turns can be found.

Off-Piste

On a powder day, going off-piste is amazing. In most resorts, the off-piste area is the ungroomed part of the mountain that is still within the resort. Off-piste boarders can experience sweeping, open trees or tight passages packed with glistening powder. Off-piste has dangers, especially in changing weather and when it has snowed heavily.

Backcountry

The backcountry offers open faces, untracked terrain, and chutes (narrow passages). But it's also dangerous. Unlike off-piste, backcountry refers to any terrain outside the resort boundaries. So there are no safety patrols and no backups if things go wrong.

BEWARE!
The backcountry is no place for beginners.

GUIDE #5

FUN PARKS

Fun parks are playgrounds for boarders. They feature obstacles and structures for boarders to ride. These can include gaps, tables, and rails. Riders of all ages can develop their skills by practicing moves at a park.

Transition

Deck

Flat bottom

QUARTER-PIPES

One side of a half-pipe, quarter-pipes are huge walls of snow. Snowboarders ride toward the wall and use the vertical part to launch themselves into the air.

Funbox

Gap

HALF-PIPES

These courses are U-shaped channels of snow. Riders use the walls of the half-pipe to get airborne and perform tricks.

So you have learned to turn and stop. You can cruise around the hill. It may be time to move on to the next two stages in your freestyle development-the powder turn and the straight air.

Learning to Jump: the Straight Air
To get in the air, you need a ramp. The snow on a ramp points skyward. You gain speed off ramps to become airborne. On a mountain, there are plenty of human-made and natural jumps.

FACE SHOT
Kicking spray up in front of you is called "getting a face shot."

5. This is the top of your air. Keep your legs prepared for landing.

4. Try to relax. Maybe do some grabs.

1. – 3. Approach the jump with your weight distributed over the board. Try to take off from a centered position.

The Powder Turn

Flying into an open, untracked powder field is about as good as life gets. So how do you do it? Powder requires a different approach from normal riding. In deeper snow, shift your weight to the tail of the board so that the nose doesn't sink. It's tiring to fall in the middle of the deep snow. But take the time to pick up the basics, and you'll never look back.

MESSY
Turning in powder is messy but a lot of fun!

6. Try to place the board in a position where it will land in one smooth, even motion with the ground.

7. Extend your legs to the ground. This will give you more time to absorb the landing.

8. Absorb the shock of landing with your knees. Keep your body weight centered. Press your whole body into the landing.

9. – 10. Simply start turning

Ask riders how often they tune their boards, and they'll probably answer "not often enough." Learn how your snowboard works. Save money and ride better and faster than your friends. You'll soon discover how to tune your board to suit your style.

Cleaning and Filing the Base

A sharp edge cuts better into the snow. First wipe the base clean with a cloth or damp rag. Start where the board meets the snow at the tip of each rail (or edge of the snowboard). Place your edge file at 90 degrees. Draw it down to the tail using sharp, short strokes. Don't force the file. Let its weight do the job.

Filing
Filing your board should look like this.

Edge File
An edge sharpener and file are essential for good riding.

GUIDE #6

WAXING

Heat an iron to a low setting. The iron should be warm enough to melt the wax but not so hot it'll burn your base. Run the iron over the base. Then rub the block of wax on to your base. Use the iron to melt and spread the wax all over the base until it is covered. Then let it cool down and set.

IRON
Ask an adult before using one of these.

Scraping

Scraping comes next. It is essential if you want your board to perform. Scrape the wax off using strong downward strokes until the excess wax has come off in flakes.

SCRAPER
A scraper gets rid of excess wax.

Pocket Tools
Pocket tools are handy in boarding emergencies.

Shred Better

A freshly waxed and edged board is faster and more responsive than one that's been neglected. Slowing down on flat spots? Wax it. Can't get enough speed or control for a trick? Sharpen those edges. Knowing as much as possible about how your board works will make you a better rider.

The lines on this half-pipe were cut with sharp edges.

Spinning is a big part of advanced freestyling. The rate of progress at this level is often amazing. All serious spinning begins with the 360. The Backside 360 is one of the easiest and safest advanced tricks to learn. Here's how it's done.

4. Now you can go for a grab.

1. You must start a spin before you take off. For a backside spin, drive your shoulder toward your back foot.

5. Keep turning those shoulders in the direction of the spin.

3. If you keep turning your upper body, you'll be committed to the Backside 360.

2. Riders wind their arms to the frontside. Then they unwind them to the backside as they approach the jump.

HANDRAILS
Riding on human-made objects is challenging.

GUIDE #7

JIBBING
Jibbing is the art of using human-made objects as snowboard terrain. Snowskating, as seen here, mixes skateboarding with snowboarding. The new sport can be useful when the weather is bad on the mountain. Snowskates look like skateboards but have a mini "ski" where the wheels would normally be.

7. – 8. By closing up or opening up your body shape, you can speed up or slow down the spin.

9. Now's the time to make any landing or flying corrections.

6. You should be able to see the landing.

10. The board still has 180 degrees yet to turn. Keep your upper body focused on the landing.

11. Bring the board to the ground. Meet the floor with a fully extended body.

12. Absorb the landing with your legs, and keep the board pointing forward.

RIDING HANDRAILS
This is a dangerous stunt.

True freeriding-riding the natural features of a mountain in a flowing style-is the ultimate form of snowboarding. It's dangerous and exciting.

Alaska

The center of the world freeriding scene is Alaska. Sea-level peaks and low temperatures allow snow to stick to incredibly steep faces. Alaska has long, almost vertical runs with a stable snowpack. Local guides help minimize the dangers of these slopes.

Freeriders

The first snowboarders to explore Alaska realized that their sport was perfect for these awesome mountains. Modern freeriders combine freestyle and freeride skills and are pushing the sport even further.

JUMPING OFF A CLIFF
The landing must be steep enough and the snow deep enough for safety. You need commitment and guts. Gravity does the rest.

The Skills to Survive

Any mistake on Alaskan terrain can be fatal. Skills that seem simple on normal terrain, such as route-finding and turning, become a matter of survival on a big face. Snowboarders who tackle these slopes must be able to ride steep slopes and jump cliffs. They must avoid crevices (cracks) and keep their nerve. Riders use cameras to plan their routes. They also train to handle sluff. Sluff is the surface snow that is released on steeper slopes. It's a surface avalanche, with the power to sweep a rider away.

GUIDE #8

TRANSPORT, ALASKAN STYLE

Getting to these mountains is expensive. Alaskan weather can leave the peaks unreachable for weeks at a time. When the weather clears, riders and guides use helicopters and snowmobiles to get to the peaks.

Helicopters
Helicopters are costly to rent. But they allow boarders to ride remote mountains.

Snowmobiles
These vehicles are great for local exploration.

GUIDE #9

THE DANGERS:

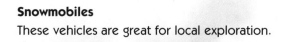

Spines
Here sluff channels itself into fast-flowing rivers of snow, creating ridges and troughs.

Cliffs
In Alaska, often the only way a rider can reach the bottom is to tackle cliffs head on.

Crevices
Crevices are deep cracks in the snow that are often thousands of feet deep.

Avalanche!

You and a friend are at an untouched field. Without warning, your friend is caught in an avalanche. You have less than half an hour to find your friend, dig him out, and get him to safety before he dies. Would you be able to take on this responsibility?

SHOVEL
Shovels are lightweight, foldable, and strong. Your shovel should be designed for shifting as much snow as possible.

AVALANCHE HIT
This avalanche hit Chamonix, France. The dots in the picture are skiers and snowboarders fleeing the slide. Fortunately, no one was killed.

The Power of Nature
Avalanches are surprising and deadly. Even experts cannot tell when they will occur. Nature can turn a perfect powder day into a nightmare in a matter of minutes.

Preparation
Every snowboarder must be armed with as much knowledge and preparation as possible. Avalanches happen to ordinary people every day. Some of the world's best, most experienced riders have been lost to these awful forces. Know-how and caution are the best defenses we have against them.

ONE MINUTE THERE'S CALM ...
... then incredible power ... then calm again.

GUIDE #10

ESSENTIAL BACKCOUNTRY KIT

Transceivers
Transceivers are your lifeline in an avalanche. They locate victims of an avalanche and act as a beacon to show the victims' positions.

Medical Kit
A medical kit is useful for small injuries.

Probe
A probe pinpoints the search. Use it to thrust deeply into the snow until you find a person.

Knowledge Is Power

The best way to protect against avalanches is to know all about them. On an avalanche course, trained guides explain how to test the snowpack. They show you how to use a transceiver properly. Untracked powder and steep, long faces are among snowboarding's most tempting thrills. But if in doubt, walk away and live to ride another day.

GOOD JUDGMENT
This rider weighed the dangers and chose to ride.

Legends of Snowboarding

Much of the appeal of snowboarding is its sheer fun. You can ride with your friends and test your limits. Like any sport, snowboarding also has its superstars.

Heroes

The sport's heroes are admired for many reasons. Most of all, they have pushed the boundaries of the sport and taken snowboarding into new territory.

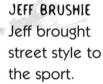

DAMIEN SANDERS
He wore the brightest clothes ever!

JEFF BRUSHIE
Jeff brought street style to the sport.

NICOLA THOST
Nicola won the first Olympic gold medal in the women's half-pipe.

CRAIG KELLY
He was one of the greatest freeriders.

JAMIE LYNN
Jamie turned snowboarding into an art form.

SHAUN PALMER
Shaun was fun and rebellious.

Terry's Tweaks and Grabs

Terry Kidwell looked at snowboarding as an extension of skateboarding. He took freestyle snowboarding from kindergarten to college in one short, dazzling period. He invented techniques that would stump many experts. Terry's tweaks and grabs and the first recorded McTwist have become legendary.

TERRY KIDWELL
He owned the first board with a nose and a tail so you could ride it backward.

Terje-The Greatest

Terje Haakonsen bought his first snowboard at age 13. By 1990 he had begun to enter pro contests. For a decade-long period, he dominated snowboarding. His tremendous style influenced all areas of snowboarding.

TERJE HAAKONSEN
A young Terje hitting the form that made him a legend.

ONBOARD
european snowboarding magazine

Issue 8
September

UK £2.75
NKR44 SMA1
BD10.75 CHF AG

summer scrapbook

Ingemar's Air

Ingemar Backman made snowboarding history in 1996 at a contest in Riksgransen, Sweden. He launched himself into the record books with the highest snowboarding air ever recorded. At 26 feet (8 meters) high, the remarkable feat made the cover of every major snowboarding magazine in the world.

MAKING HISTORY
Ingemar Backman became the most talked about snowboarder ever.

Brimmer, Larry Dane. *Snowboarding.* New York: Franklin Watts, 1997.

Carlson, Julia. *A Woman's Guide to Snowboarding.* Camden, ME: Ragged Mountain Press, 1999.

Daniells, Greg. *Let it Rip: The Ultimate Guide to Snowboarding.* Edison, NJ: Chartwell Books, 1997.

Fabbro, Mike. *Snowboarding: The Ultimate Freeride.* Toronto: McClelland & Stewart, 1996.

Hayhurst, Chris. *Snowboarding: Shred the Powder.* New York: Rosen Central, 1999.

Iguchi, Bryan. *The Young Snowboarder.* New York: DK Publishing, 1997.

Malthouse, Becci. *Snowboarding.* Hauppauge, NY: Barron's Educational Series, 1998.

Masoff, Joy. *Snowboard!* Washington, D.C.: National Geographic, 2002.

Maurer, Tracy Nelson. *Snowboarding.* Vero Beach, FL: Rourke Publishing, 2002.

Older, Effin. *Snowboarding.* Mechanicsburg, PA: Stackpole Books, 1999.

Sullivan, George. *Snowboarding.* New York: Cobblehill Books, 1997.

Van Tilburg, Christopher. *Backcountry Snowboarding.* Seattle, WA: The Mountaineers, 1998.

WEBSITES

American Association of Snowboard Instructors
 <http://www.aasi.org>
Boarderzone
 <http://boarderzone.com/>
Snowboardermag.com
 <http://www.snowboardermag.com/>
Snowboarding
 <http://www.snowboarding.com/>
Snowboarding^2
 <http://www.snowboarding2.com>
Transworld Snowboarding
 <http://www.transworldsnowboarding.com/snow/>
United States of America Snowboard Association
 <http://www.usasa.org/>
United States Ski and Snowboard Association
 <http://www.ussnowboard.com>

Glossary

air: any trick that involves leaving the ground on a snowboard. "Catching air" means becoming airborne.

chute: a steep, narrow corridor of snow between two bands of rock

freeriding: using the natural features of a mountain from top to bottom in a flowing, fluid style. Sometimes also known as "top-to-bottom" snowboarding.

grab: a trick where a rider grabs the board while getting air, for balance and extra style. There are many different types of grabs.

heli-boarding: using a helicopter to access mountains and terrain that cannot be reached in any other way. Expensive and at times dangerous, heli-boarding is one of the most exhilarating types of snowboarding.

indy: grabbing the board between the bindings on the toe edge with the back hand

mute: a simple grab, with the front hand between the bindings on the toe edge

pipe: usually refers to a half-pipe, a channel cut into the snow comprising two transitioned walls leading to a vertical section. A quarter-pipe has only one transitional wall.

powder: light, freshly fallen snow that has not yet been ridden on

roast beef: a trick in which the rider grabs the board between the bindings on the heel edge, passing the back hand through the legs

stalefish: a trick where a rider grabs the board between the bindings on the heel edge with the back hand

terrain park: a fun park for freestyle snowboarding, made up of handrails, half-pipes, and jumps

transition: where a half-pipe or quarter-pipe wall goes from flat to vertical in a smooth, gradual arc

tweaking: when a rider exaggerates a grab by contorting the body (for example, by straightening the front leg) to emphasize the control he or she has

ROCK CLIMBING

First American edition published in 2004
by LernerSports

This book is available in two editions:
Library binding by LernerSports
Soft cover by First Avenue Editions
Imprints of Lerner Publishing Group
241 First Avenue North
Minneapolis, MN 55401 U.S.A.

Website address: www.lernerbooks.com

Designed and produced by:
David West 🏃 Children's Books
7 Princeton Court
55 Felsham Road
London, England

Designer: Gary Jeffrey
Editor: James Pickering
Picture Research: Carlotta Cooper

Library of Congress Cataloging-in-Publication Data

Oxlade, Chris.
  Rock climbing/ by Chris Oxlade.—1st American ed.
  p. cm.—(Extreme Sports)
  Includes index.
  Summary: Provides an introduction to the sport of
rock climbing, along with information on the
sport's history, styles of climbing, equipment,
techniques, popular sites for climbing, and some of
the dangers.
  ISBN: 0–8225–1240–8 (lib. bdg.)
  ISBN: 0–8225–1190–8 (pbk.)
  1. Rock climbing—Juvenile Literature. [1. Rock
climbing.] I. Title. II. Extreme sports (Minneapolis,
Minn.)
GV200.2 .O95 2004
796.52'23—dc21   2002013601
Bound in the United States of America
1 2 3 4 5 6 – OS – 09 08 07 06 05 04

PHOTO CREDITS :
Abbreviations: t-top, m-middle, b-bottom, r-right,
l-left, c-center.

Front cover - Corbis. 3, 7br, 15t & m, 16r, 17 both,
18, 18-19, 20 both, 26-27, 28t - Buzz Pictures. 4-5,
8-9b, 12l, 14l, 16l, 23tr & bl, 24l, 25t, 30 - Corbis
Images. 6t & b, 6-7, 7tr & m, 10b, 11bl, 21, 22-
23, 24tr (John Cleare), 8-9t (Bill March), 10t (Chris
Craggs), 22, 29l (Ian Smith), 29r (Dave Simmonite)
- Mountain Camera Picture Library. 5, 8 both, 9,
11tl & r, 14r, 19, 20-21, 23br, 24br, 25m & b, 27,
28b - Stockshot. 12br - Scarpa / The Mountain
Boot Co. Ltd. 13 all - Petzl / Lyon Equipment Ltd.

The author and publishers have made every effort
to ensure that the information in this book is
accurate. However, no responsibility can be
accepted by the author or publishers for any errors,
inaccuracies, or omissions. This book is not a guide
to rock climbing or a manual of climbing
techniques. No responsibility can be accepted by
the author or publishers for any accident or
damages sustained by climbers for whatever reason.
In this book you will see climbers without helmets.
The author and publishers strongly recommend the
use of helmets by all climbers.

*An explanation of difficult words can be
found in the glossary on page 31.*

extreme sports

ROCK CLIMBING

Chris Oxlade

LERNER SPORTS
AN IMPRINT OF LERNER PUBLISHING GROUP

CONTENTS

ACCEPTING THE RISKS
Rock climbing has many risk factors. Most climbers are not foolish. If the risks are too great, they don't climb.

Introduction

Imagine yourself high above the ground on a steep rock face. You climb upward, holding on only by your fingertips and the sticky rubber on your climbing shoes. Even though you are protected by a rope, your brain urges you not to fall. Your arms are tired. But your skill and courage eventually carry you to the top of the rock. Success!

The question climbers are asked most often by nonclimbers is "why do you climb?" For some, it's the thrill of success when they complete a scary climb. For other climbers, it's the physical challenge, a love of the outdoors, or the fun of competition. Every style of climbing has its own unique challenges and rewards.

WARNING!
ROCK CLIMBING CAN BE AN **EXTREMELY DANGEROUS** SPORT. DO NOT TRY ANY FORM OF ROCK CLIMBING WITHOUT **PROFESSIONAL SUPERVISION**.

ADVENTUROUS CLIMBING
Climbers who climb mountains or seacliffs enjoy the adventure. They rely on themselves to avoid trouble.

Rock Climbing History

People have probably climbed rocks for thousands of years. But rock climbing as a sport began only just over a century ago.

The Birth of Rock Climbing

Rock climbing is part of alpinism, or mountain climbing. Alpinism began in the 1800s. It is named after the Alps, a mountain range in Europe. British alpinists began climbing small rock faces in Britain as training for their vacations in the Alps. They enjoyed it so much that the sport of rock climbing was born!

HEMP ROPE

Early climbers used ropes made from a plant called hemp. The ropes often broke when climbers fell!

GIUSTO GERVASUTTI

Italian Giusto Gervasutti scaled many hard routes in the eastern Alps. He died in 1946 rappelling (coming down from a climb).

THE FIRST ROCK CLIMB

One of the first examples of rock climbing for fun took place in 1886. W.P. Haskett-Smith climbed Napes Needle, a rock pillar in England.

ARTIFICIAL CLIMBS
Climbing walls were developed in the 1970s as places to train. Since then they have evolved into impressive structures with rocklike features.

Equipment and Technique
Climbers developed specialized equipment in the 1950s. Rubber-soled boots, nylon ropes, and carabiners (metal links) made climbing much safer. The new gear allowed climbers to try harder routes.

JOE BROWN
Joe Brown was the leading British rock climber of the 1950s and 1960s. He led more than 600 new routes.

BEN MOON
Modern-day climber Ben Moon spends most of his life clinging to boulders.

New Branches
The popularity of rock climbing has grown in the last twenty years. New branches of the sport—such as bouldering and competition climbing—provide new challenges.

Climbing Styles

Rock climbing has several different branches. Each branch has its own thrills and needs different skills. Many climbers try different branches of the sport. Some climbers specialize in just one branch.

AID CLIMBING
An aid climber on a big wall rests on his gear.

Lead Climbing

Most climbs are done in teams. One climber (called the leader) climbs up first. The leader clips the rope through equipment that's attached to the rock. The other climber (called the second or belayer) feeds out the rope. That climber holds the rope tightly in case the leader falls off. This process is called belaying.

LEADER AND BELAYER
The leader relies on the rope and the belayer (the second) to avoid hitting the ground.

Bouldering

Boulderers climb without ropes on boulders or rock edges. They don't usually go more than 15 feet (about 5 meters) off the ground. Any higher could mean serious injury.

THE BOULDERING SCENE
Boulder climbs are normally short and hard. They have two or three very difficult moves. A thick foam mat and another climber "spotting" help to break any fall.

Free and Aid

Most climbing is free climbing. The climber uses hands and feet to hold on and move up the rock. Free climbers use ropes but only to save them if they fall.

The opposite of free climbing is aid climbing. Aid climbers climb up ropes that are already attached to the rock. Aid climbing techniques are used on climbs that would be impossible to free climb.

SOLO CLIMBING

"Soloing" is ropeless climbing on high rock faces. It can have deadly results if anything goes wrong.

ROUTES AND CRACKS

Climbers normally follow a path, or route, up the rock. This route follows a crack.

Lead climbers use ropes and clip them to the rock. The equipment, called protection, protects the leader against long, dangerous falls. There are two forms of lead climbing—traditional and sports.

Leading a Traditional Route

In traditional (or trad) climbing, the leader places protection equipment into cracks in the rock while climbing. This sort of protection is called leader-placed protection. The second climber takes out the protection as he or she passes it. On some trad routes, there may be few chances for placing protection. These routes can be scary and more dangerous.

A RUNNING BELAY
The pieces of protection with the rope clipped through them are called running belays or runners.

ON A TRAD ROUTE
A traditional leader needs experience to decide how often to put in protection and to place it securely.

Leading a Sports Route

In sports climbing, steel rings are already bolted into the rock every few feet. The leader simply clips the rope to each ring. Sports routes (or "bolted" routes) are put up in places where traditional protection is impossible to place.

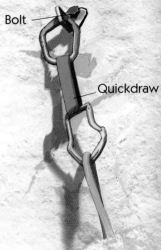

Bolt

Quickdraw

A sports climber clips one end of a quickdraw to the bolt and clips the rope through the other end.

TRAVELING LIGHT
A sports route requires very little equipment, just a supply of bolt connections, known as quickdraws.

Top and Bottom Roping

In top roping and bottom roping, the climber is protected from falling by a rope leading to a secure anchor at the top of the route. For top roping, the belayer sits at the top of the route. For bottom roping, the belayer stands at the bottom.

PRACTICE MAKES PERFECT
Top roping (right) and bottom roping (left) are used for beginners and for practicing new routes.

Basic Climbing Equipment

Each branch of climbing needs different equipment. Boulderers often use just a pair of rock shoes and a chalk bag. Trad climbers need harnesses, ropes, belay devices, and lots of protection equipment.

Equipment to Wear

You can climb in any clothes, as long as they allow free movement and fit weather conditions. A harness is worn over clothing. Most climbers wear sit harnesses. Very young climbers and aid climbers should wear full body harnesses.

SIT HARNESS

Belay loop

Loops for holding gear

Waistbelt with padding for comfort

Buckles to fasten loops

Leg loops

CHALKING UP

Climbers put powdered chalk on their hands to dry up sweat and to increase grip.

STICKY SHOES

Rock shoes have a rubber sole that gives amazing grip on the steepest rock.

SCARPA

HEAD PROTECTION
A helmet protects the head from falling rocks and during a fall.

KNOW THE ROPES
Standard climbing ropes are 164 feet (50 meters) long. An inner nylon core gives the rope strength. The outer layer protects the core.

More Gear
Climbing ropes are slightly stretchy. A stretchy rope stops a climber's fall gradually, not suddenly. A carabiner is a strong metal hoop with an opening called a gate.

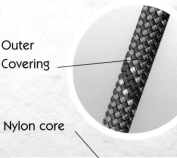

Outer Covering

Nylon core

CARABINERS
This type of carabiner is called a snap-link. Locking carabiners have a mechanism that stops the gate from opening accidentally.

A BELAY DEVICE
A belay device is always attached to a belayer's harness with a locking carabiner.

SLINGS AND QUICKDRAWS
A sling is a loop of strong nylon tape. A quickdraw (or extender) consists of a short sling that joins two snap-link carabiners.

13

Techniques and Holds

Technique is as important as strength when tackling rock faces. Good technique helps a climber to move well and to keep up energy levels.

Feet and Footwork

Beginners tend to climb with their arms, dragging their legs behind them. Experienced climbers know that the secret of good climbing is to keep their weight on their feet. They push upward with their strong leg muscles, rather than pulling up with their arms.

TRUST YOUR FEET
Weight on the feet helps shoes grip holds and steep rock.

KEEPING BALANCE
On steep slabs, staying upright is better than leaning inward. This keeps the weight on the feet. It helps to stop the feet slipping off.

GUIDE #3

BASIC FOOTHOLDS

There are two basic ways of using feet in climbing— edging and smearing.

1. Edging is standing on small ledges with the side of a shoe.

2. Smearing is putting the sole of a shoe against the rock where there is no foothold.

CLIMBING SIDEWAYS

This climber is climbing sideways, called traversing. Sometimes you have to traverse or down-climb if you've gotten stuck.

TINY HOLDS

Tiny holds like this are called crimps.

Handholds

On sloping rock, climbers tend to use their hands only for balance. On overhanging rock, they have to use them to hang on. Climbers have different names for different types of holds, such as jugs, slopers, pockets, crimps, and pinches.

GUIDE #4

JAMMING

Some types of rock have lots of cracks in them. Jamming is a way of holding on by jamming a hand or fist into a crack.

Finger Jam

Hand Jam

Fist Jam

Some routes go along the underside of an overhang. Others have very few handholds or footholds. On these routes, climbers have to use creative techniques to climb upward. They need strength, endurance, and focus.

LAYBACKING
Laybacking is leaning out to keep feet pressed against the rock.

Climbing Moves
Laybacking is a technique that uses both hands and feet on the same upright feature. Bridging is putting one foot on each wall of a corner. It's useful for resting tired arms. Other techniques include mantleshelfing, chimneying, heel hooks, and dynos.

ARÊTE CLIMBING
Laybacking is often the only way to climb an arête (sharp ridge).

GUIDE #5

MANTLESHELFING
Mantleshelfing is used when there are no holds on or above a ledge.

1. The climber holds the edge of the ledge and walks feet up.

2. The climber pushes down on the ledge and straightens the arms.

3. The climber lifts one foot on to the ledge and then rocks forward to stand up.

JUMPING FOR HOLDS
Sometimes, it is so far between handholds that the only way to get up is to jump! This is called dynoing.

Don't Get Gripped
Success on traditional routes depends on a cool head as much as good technique. Panicking, or getting "gripped," only makes a fall more likely.

Training and Injuries
Climbers train to build strength and endurance. Strong fingers and arms are needed to grip small holds and to pull up. Endurance is needed to hang on for long periods. Climbers also stretch and warm up before climbing to prevent injuries.

CHIMNEYING
This climber is wedging himself in a chimney by pressing his back and feet on to opposite walls.

Climbing a Route

Let's see how a pair of climbers climbs a bolted sports route. The bolts are already placed in the rock. Note the roles and moves of the leader and the second.

Leading and Seconding

The leader climbs first, clipping the rope through the bolted protection. The second belays from below. At the top of the route, the leader becomes the belayer. He or she creates a belay by tying securely to the bolts in the rock. Next the second climbs the route, protected from above by the leader.

CLIPPING BOLTS
This climber has clipped one bolt and heads to the next one.

SINGLEHANDED
The leader has clipped a quickdraw to the bolt and will clip the rope to it.

GUIDE #6

SPORTS ROUTE SEQUENCE
Short sports routes often end partway up a rock face. The climber follows the bolts up to the anchor. Then the belayer lowers the climber back to the ground.

Multipitch Routes

If a route is longer than the length of a rope, it is climbed in sections called pitches. Each pitch ends at a convenient place, such as a ledge. There, the leader ties to the rock and belays up the second.

FALLING OFF
If climbers are about to fall, they push away from the rock to avoid hitting it.

A MULTIPITCH ROUTE
Climbers often take turns leading pitches of a multipitch route.

Traditional Leading

As on a trad route, the leader climbs first to put protection into the rock.

RACKING UP
A climber's protection gear, a rack, is carried on a harness or a shoulder strap

Leader-Placed Protection

On a traditional route, the leader carries the protection gear. He or she brings nuts, hexes, camming devices, and slings. During the climb, the leader looks for cracks and other features where protection equipment will fit. It takes practice to place protection securely, so that the gear will not pull out of the rock if the climber falls. Removing the protection gear is the job of the second climber.

PLACING PROTECTION
A climber tries to find the best spot to place a wired nut.

BUILDING A BELAY
At the top of a pitch, the leader builds a belay by tying onto an anchor (like a rock or a sturdy tree) and then belays the second up.

GUIDE #7
LEADER-PLACED PROTECTION

Nuts
Nuts wedge into small cracks. The rope clips to the wire hoop.

Camming devices
These have toothed parts that expand to fit in cracks. Pulling the cam makes it jam in more tightly.

Slings
Slings are loops of nylon. They are threaded around rock spikes and jammed boulders.

Hexes
Hexes are six-sided metal tubes that jam into cracks.

Getting Down

If climbers can't walk from the top of a climb, they have to rappel. Rappelling is sliding down a rope that's tied to an anchor at the top of a rock face. It may take several rappels to get down a high rock face.

RAPPELLING DOWN
Rappelling is great fun, but be careful not to go too fast or to slide off the end of the rope in midair. Rappelling can be more dangerous than climbing.

21

You can climb anywhere there's a surface that can be scaled. Popular spots are boulders, old quarries, crags, seacliffs, and rock faces.

SEA STACK CLIMBING
Giant columns of rock, called sea stacks, are a big challenge. The first problem is reaching the base!

Adventure Climbing

More adventurous climbers head for remote mountain crags or towering seacliffs. Falling off isn't the only danger. The rock may be loose. Routes may be hard to follow. The weather may turn bad. Climbers must be prepared to stay out of trouble. Big waves and rising tides are extra hazards on seacliffs.

PROBLEMS
Even the smallest outcrops of rock can offer tough and entertaining bouldering problems.

CLIMBING WALLS
Walls have sections for bouldering, bottom roping, and lead climbing. Walls are popular with beginners. Experienced climbers use them to keep up their strength and endurance between climbs.

CLIMBING INDOORS
Indoor climbing walls are made from flat wooden or fiberglass panels with colored holds.

Big Wall Climbing

Perhaps the most adventurous of all is "big-wall" climbing. Big walls are vertical rock faces often more than 3,000 feet (1,000 meters) high. Routes can take many days to complete. El Capitan is a wall of granite half a mile (one kilometer) high in California's Yosemite Valley. Climbers go up it by free climbing or aid climbing. Climbing El Capitan may take several days to complete.

CALIFORNIA'S BIG WALL
Crispin Waddy relaxes on top of the Texas Flake, more than 1,200 feet (366 meters) up on El Capitan.

Luckily, most countries have rocks to climb. Some have more than others! In the last ten years or so, climbers have begun to explore every corner of the world in search of new crags and cliffs.

North America

The United States has the greatest range of climbing of any country. Yosemite offers climbing on smaller crags and boulders. Other popular places are Joshua Tree near Los Angeles, California, and the canyons in the Rockies.

JOSHUA TREE
There are over 4,500 climbing routes within an area of about 100,000 acres at Joshua Tree National Park.

ENGLISH GRITSTONE
Northern England has crags of rough stone, with long cracks and rounded edges.

SUN, SEA, AND CLIMBS IN ASIA
If it's sun and sea you're after, plus great climbing, head for Asia. In Thailand, there are exciting bolted sports routes on dramatic cliffs.

ALPINE ROCK

The Alps offer big climbs in spectacular scenery. There are often glaciers (moving ice masses) to cross to reach the base.

Europe

Britain has a huge variety of mountain crags, low rocky outcrops, and high seacliffs. Most routes are climbed in traditional style. Some cliffs in Britain have hard, technical bolted sports routes. There are huge mountain crags in the Alps. France and Spain are the homes of sports climbing. There, climbers can tackle thousands of bolted routes.

SPANISH ROCK

Spain's Costa Blanca has high-quality sports routes near popular tourist resorts.

AUSTRALIA

Mount Arapiles in Victoria, Australia, has several miles of sandstone cliffs. They make up one of the best crags in the world. The Blue Mountains near Sydney are also a popular sport-climbing spot.

QUITE REMARKABLE

At Remarkable Rocks, South Australia, nature has turned the rock into incredible shapes.

25

Grades, Guides, and Ethics

Every route and boulder that is climbed is given a grade. The grade tells other climbers how hard it is to climb. Different countries have their own grading systems. They also have their own unwritten rules (called ethics).

Grades around the World
Routes are given a grade (and a name) by the first person to climb them. The grade is a measure of the route's difficulty.

	BRITAIN		USA	FRANCE
MODERATE			5.2	1
DIFFICULT			5.3	2
VERY DIFFICULT			5.4	3
SEVERE		4a	5.5	4
	HARD SEVERE	4b	5.6	5
			5.7	
	VERY SEVERE	4c		
HARD VERY SEVERE		5a	5.8	5+
			5.9	
EXTREME 1		5b	5.10a	6a
			5.10b	6a+
EXTREME 2		5c	5.10c	6b
			5.10d	6b+
			5.11a	6c
		6a	5.11b	6c+
EXTREME 3	EXTREME 4		5.11c	7a
			5.11d	7a+
	EXTREME 5	6b	5.12a	7b
			5.12b	7b+
			5.12c	7c
		6c	5.12d	7c+
			5.13a	8a
EXTREME 6-9			5.13b	8a+
		7a	5.13c	8b
			5.13d	8b+
		7b	5.14a	8c

WORLD GRADES
This chart compares British, North American, and French grading systems.

Guide books contain
names, grades, and
descriptions of
routes. Photos,
diagrams, and maps
help climbers find
their way around.

Mollywash Wall

99 High Ridge 10m E15b   (1976)
The protected bulge right of Guardian crack is climbed
trending diagonally leftwards. A strong approach is needed.
It has been frequently claimed over the last few years and
is therefore known by a multiplicity of names. This is the proper
name, or is it?

100 The Scraper 8m VS 4c   (1958- 1964)
A few metres right is a nice jamming crack that slices
a nice little arrete. Well named.

101 Lay Back 6m HS 4a   (1956- 1964)
"Layback and think of England" as they say. A well defined
crack leads to a layback below the overhang.

102 Ring my Dell 8m E4 6b   (1986)
Why not climb the right edge of the next buttress. The
bulge above is exciting.

103 Ringu 10m VD   (1958- 1963)
Just right are two splits. The left hand one is undercut on
it's base.

104 Ming Peice 10m HVS 6a   (1992)
The skinny face on the right leads to a hand move and a side
runner and on to an easy finish.

105 Ming Climb 11m VD   (1933- 1952)
The second crack goes to a platform then on above.

106 Ming's Chimney 7m VD   (1935- 1952)
Ascend to the next cleft.

Climbing Ethics

Climbing is a sport without official rules. Different
styles of climbing and different countries have their
own ethics. Most climbers climb under strict
standards. They have to climb a route in one try, and
place protection on the way. Climbers can't rest on
the rope or practice moves beforehand.

HANGING PRACTICE
Some climbers
practice routes
on a top
rope before
leading them.

BOLTING A ROUTE
Bolting is usual in
some places. But in others,
local climbers want the rock
to remain untouched.

Climbing is a naturally competitive sport. There's usually rivalry between friends as they try new routes or boulder problems. Formal climbing competition began in the 1980s on specially built climbing walls.

Three Events

Competition climbing tests a climber's technique, strength, and ability. Three different competition events test difficulty, speed, and bouldering. In the difficulty event, climbers lead a bolted route without seeing it first. In the speed event, climbers race to the top. In the bouldering event, climbers complete as many problems as possible.

BEST IN THE WORLD
The Chamonix World Cup climbing competition is held in France.

BOULDERING EVENT
Competitors in the bouldering event try to complete a series of boulder problems in as few tries as possible.

Amateurs and Pros

You don't have to be an expert climber to enter a competition. Competitions have junior, youth, and adult levels. They start with informal events at local climbing walls. The hardest test is the World Cup. The world's top competition climbers earn a living from prize money and sponsorship (money from promoting brands of equipment).

DIFFICULTY EVENT

An expert climber sets a route by putting bolt-on holds onto the climbing wall. The climber who reaches the highest point on the route wins.

STEEP OVERHANGS
Competition routes are normally on steep overhangs. The holds are small and far apart.

Further Reading & Websites

FURTHER READING

Armentrout, David. *Climbing*. Vero Beach, FL: The Rourke Press, 1998.

Brimner, Larry Dane. *Rock Climbing*. New York: Franklin Watts, 1997.

Creasey, Malcolm. *Rock Climbing: Moving up the Grades*. New York: Anness Publishing, 2000.

Hattingh, Garth. *Rock & Wall Climbing*. Mechanicsburg, PA: Stackpole Books, 2000.

Joyce, Gary. *Climbing with Children*. Birmingham, AL: Menasha Ridge Press, 1996.

Lewis, Peter. *Toproping*. Helena, MT: Falcon Press Publishing Co., 1998.

Long, John. *Gym Climb*. Evergreen, CO: Chockstone Press, 1994.

Luebben, Craig. *How to Rappel!* Helena, MT: Falcon Press Publishing Co., 1998.

Roberts, Jeremy. *Rock & Ice Climbing: Top the Tower*. New York: Rosen Central, 2000.

Twight, Mark F. *Extreme Alpinism*. Seattle, WA: The Mountaineers, 1999.

Walker, Kevin. *Learn Rock Climbing in a Weekend*. New York: Alfred A. Knopf, 1992.

WEBSITES

Climbing Online
  <http://www.climbing.com/>
Climbing Tools & Terms
  <http://www.climbing.apollo.lv/frm _e2.htm>
Rock & Ice
  <http://www.rockandice.com/>
Rockclimbing.com
  <http://www.rockclimbing.com/>
RockList.com
  <http://www.rocklist.com/>
The American Alpine Club
  <http://www.americanalpineclub. org/index htm>
The American Safe Climbing Association
  <http://www.safeclimbing.org/>
The National Park Service Park Net
  <http://www.nps.gov/>

All the Internet addresses (URLs) given in this book were valid at the time of going to press. However, due to the dynamic nature of the Internet, some addresses or content may have changed, or sites may have ceased to exist since publication. While the author and publishers regret any inconvenience this may cause readers, no responsibility for any such changes can be accepted by either the author or the publishers.

Glossary

belay: a place on a ledge or the top of a cliff where a climber attaches to the rock so that he or she can safely belay another climber

belayer: a person who controls the rope as a climber climbs, feeding it out and taking it in. If the climber falls, the belayer grips the rope to prevent the climber from falling too far.

bolt: a piece of steel with a ring on the end. It is screwed into the rock face.

bouldering: climbing without ropes close to the ground on large boulders or at the bottom of cliffs

carabiner: an oval or pear-shaped metal ring, used for clipping together other pieces of equipment, such as ropes and nuts

lead climbing: a style of climbing where the climber clips the rope to protection to stop him or her from falling too far

leader: the climber who climbs first and clips the rope into protection

protection: equipment that climbers clip a rope through as they climb. On sports routes, the protection is bolts already in the rock. On traditional routes, it is placed by the climber.

quickdraw: a piece of equipment made up of two carabiners connected with a short nylon sling

rack: a climber's protection gear, carried on a harness or a shoulder strap

running belay (or runner): a bolt or piece of leader-placed protection with the climbing rope clipped through it so that the rope can run up and down

second: the climber who climbs second, belayed from above by the leader. The second removes the rope from protection.

soloing: climbing high routes without using a rope for protection

sports climbing: climbing on routes that are protected by a line of bolts already attached to the rock

traditional (trad) climbing: climbing on routes where there are no pre-attached bolts. In trad climbing, the leader places protection into cracks and clips the rope through it.